A Note to Parents

DK READERS is a compelling program for beginning readers, designed in conjunction with leading literacy experts, including Dr. Linda Gambrell, Distinguished Professor of Education at Clemson University. Dr. Gambrell has served as President of the National Reading Conference, the College Reading Association, and the International Reading Association.

Beautiful illustrations and superb full-color photographs combine with engaging, easy-to-read stories to offer a fresh approach to each subject in the series. Each DK READER is guaranteed to capture a child's interest while developing his or her reading skills, general knowledge, and love of reading.

The five levels of DK READERS are aimed at different reading abilities, enabling you to choose the books that are exactly right for your child:

Pre-level 1: Learning to read
Level 1: Beginning to read
Level 2: Beginning to read alone
Level 3: Reading alone
Level 4: Proficient readers

The "normal" age at which a child begins to read can be anywhere from three to eight years old. Adult participation through the lower levels is very helpful for providing encouragement, discussing storylines, and sounding out unfamiliar words.

No matter which level you select, you can be sure that you are helping your child learn to read, then read to learn!

LONDON, NEW YORK, MUNICH,
MELBOURNE, AND DELHI

DK LONDON
Series Editor Deborah Lock
US Senior Editor Shannon Beatty
Project Art Editor Hoa Luc
Producers, Pre-production
Francesca Wardell, Vikki Nousiainen
Illustrator Hoa Luc

Reading Consultant
Linda Gambrell, Ph.D.

DK DELHI
Editor Nandini Gupta
Assistant Art Editor Yamini Panwar
DTP Designers Anita Yadav, Vijay Kandwal
Picture Researcher Sumedha Chopra
Deputy Managing Editor Soma B. Chowdhury

First American Edition, 2014
Published in the United States by DK Publishing
345 Hudson Street, New York, New York 10014

14 15 16 17 18 10 9 8 7 6 5 4 3
003—256578—July/14

Published in Great Britain by Dorling Kindersley Limited.

A catalog record for this book is available from the Library of Congress.

ISBN: 978-1-4654-1999-6 (Paperback)
ISBN: 978-1-4654-1998-9 (Hardcover)

DK books are available at special discounts when purchased in bulk for sales promotions, premiums, fund-raising, or educational use.
For details, contact:
DK Publishing Special Markets
345 Hudson Street, New York, New York 10014
SpecialSales@dk.com

Printed and bound in China by
South China Printing Company

The publisher would like to thank the following for their kind permission to reproduce their photographs:
(Key: a=above, b=below/bottom, c=center, l=left, r=right, t=top)
5 Dreamstime.com: Andylid (br). **12 Alamy Images:** John Eccles (bc). **15 Fotolia:** Stefan Andronache (br). **20 Fotolia:** Eric Isselee (cl); Viorel Sima (cr). **21 Fotolia:** Eric Isselee (cl). **22 Getty Images:** OrangeDukeProductions/E+ (bl) **23 Getty Images:** Gyro Photography / Amanaimagesrf (tc). **24 Fotolia:** Willee Cole (cl); Eric Isselee (cb); Nikola Spasenoski (bc). **27 Getty Images:** Image Source (br). **29 Dorling Kindersley:** Richbourne Kennels (l). **30 Dreamstime.com:** Andylid (tl), Excentro (cl), Leremy (clb); **Getty Images:** OrangeDukeProductions/E+ (cla)
Jacket images: Front cover: Alamy Images: LJSphotography (l); **Dreamstime.com:** Red2000 (br)

Discover more at
www.dk.com

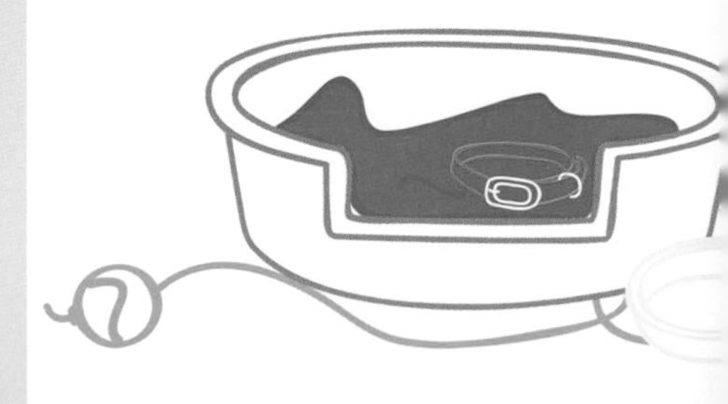

DK READERS

Playful Puppy

Written by Charlotte Hicks

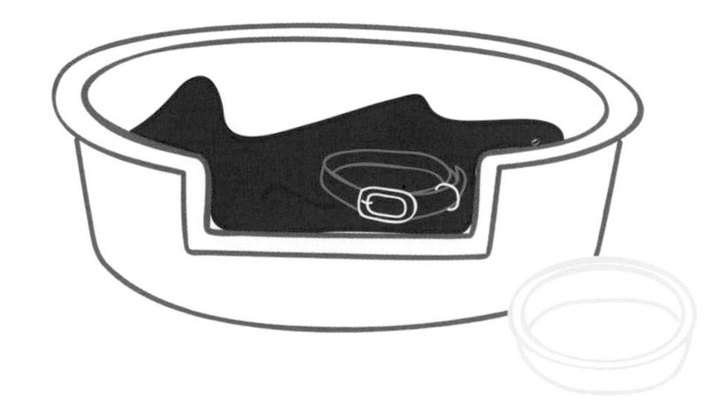

Holly had been waiting

for this day for a very long time.

She could not believe her dream

was about to come true.

Everything was ready.

There was only one thing left

to check off the list...

her new puppy!

checklist

Puppy Checklist

This is a checklist of things that are needed for taking care of a puppy.

- [ ] puppy
- [x] puppy food
- [x] bed

Holly's mom and dad

came into the living room.

Mom was carrying

a big, blue box.

Holly slowly opened the lid

and out jumped

her new best friend!

"I will call him Woody,"

said Holly.

"That is a good name,"

said Dad.

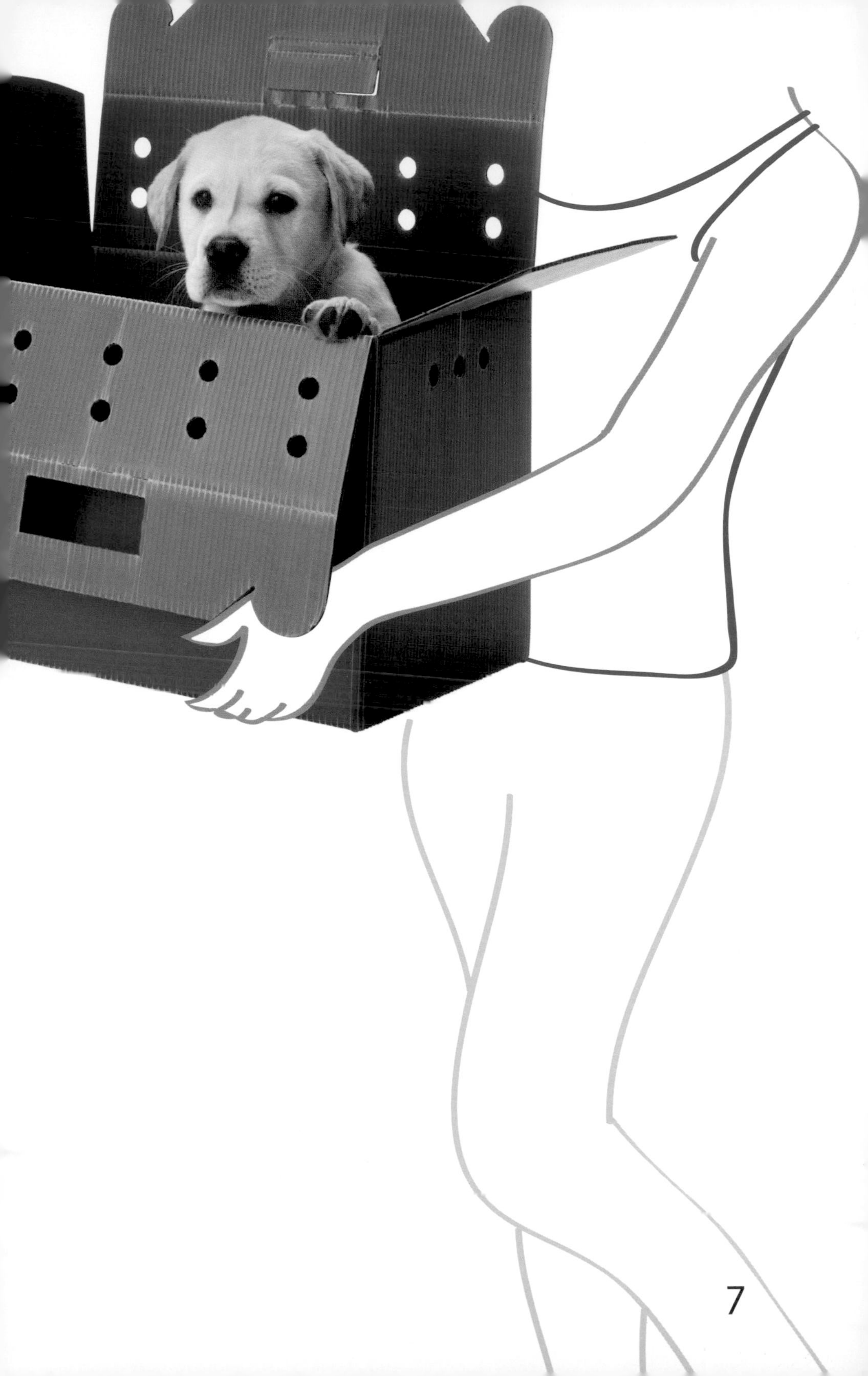

Woody saw Dad's shoe

on the floor.

Chew, chew, chew!

"Stop that, you playful puppy!"

said Dad.

Woody saw Mom's lunch

on the table.

Munch, munch, munch!

"Stop that, you playful puppy!"

called Mom.

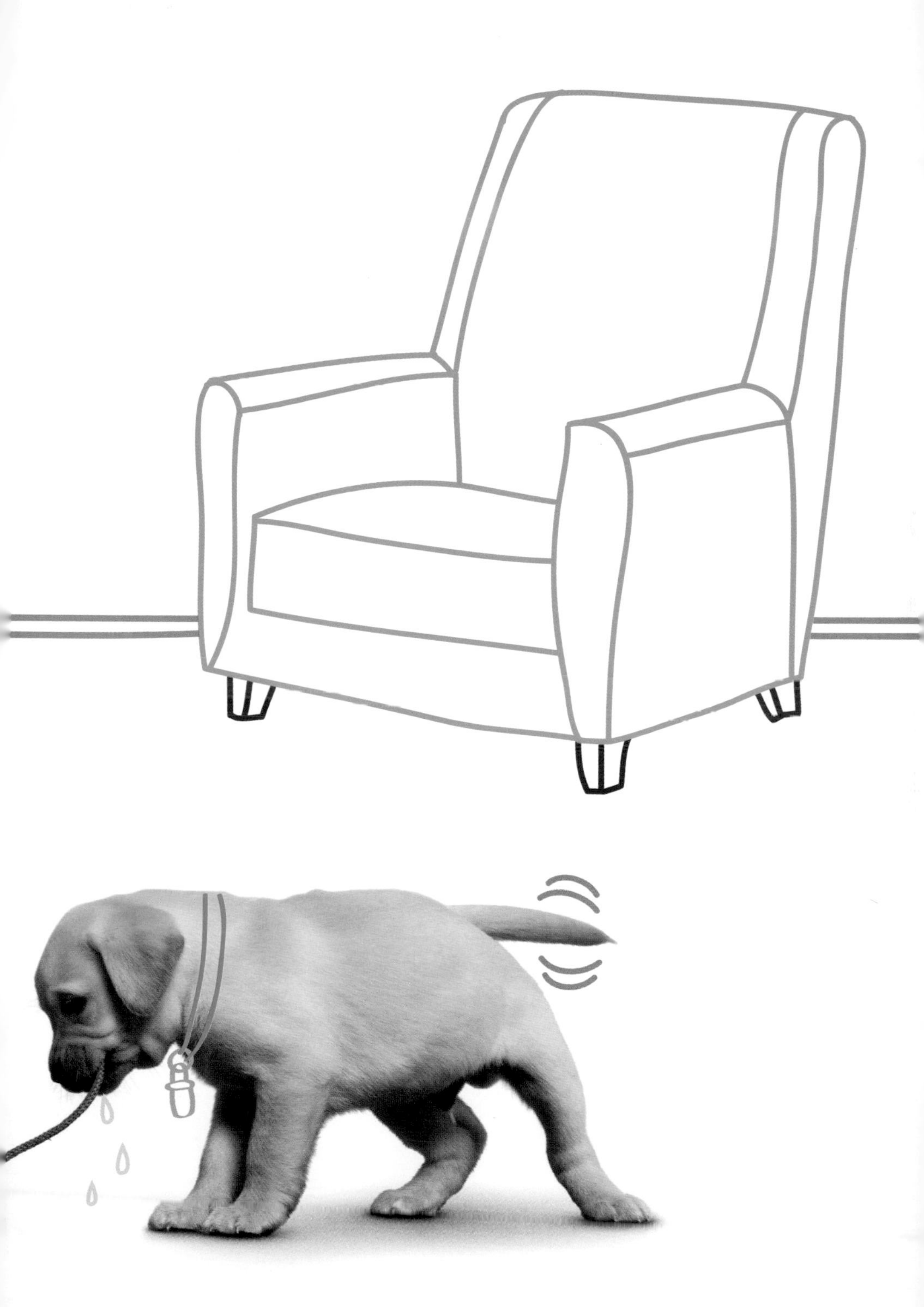

Holly's big sister, Megan,

had left her hat

on the floor.

Woody grabbed the hat

and ran out the door

to the backyard.

"That playful puppy

needs to be trained!"

cried Megan.

training

Holly went out to the backyard

to train Woody.

"Woody, sit!" said Holly.

"Woof, woof!" barked Woody.

He rolled on the grass and

wagged his tail.

"Woody, come!" called Holly,

but Woody had seen Buster,

the rabbit, hopping around

the yard.

Woody wanted to play with him.

He chased him around and around.

"Come here, you playful puppy!"

shouted Holly.

Suddenly Holly heard

a great big SPLASH!

Woody had jumped

into the pond.

He was swimming

with the fish!

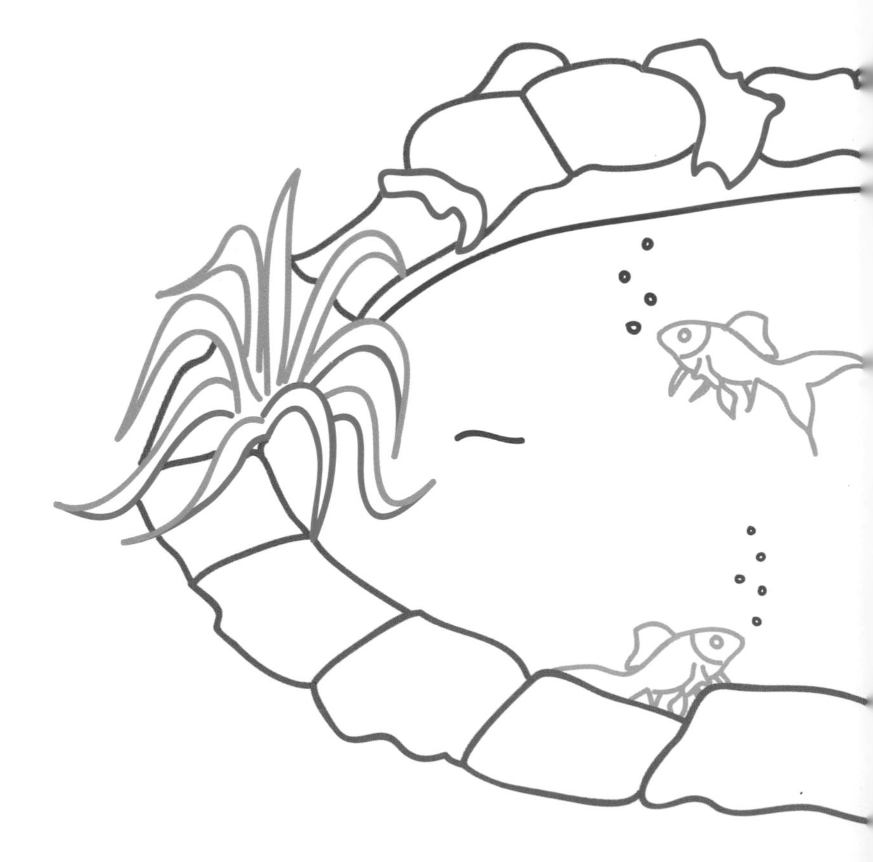

"What am I going to do with you?"

asked Holly, laughing.

On Saturday, there was a fair

in the town square.

Holly played a game and

won a teddy bear.

Megan had fun

on the bouncy castle.

Woody licked a boy's ice-cream cone!

There was going to be
a dog show at the fair.
Everyone was very excited.

Dogs of all shapes and sizes

had come to the fair

with their owners.

There were lots of prizes to be won.

The judge came over

to look at Woody.

"Be a good boy," said Holly.

His tail began to wag.

Oh no!

Woody jumped up at the judge.

He left dirty paw prints

on her new dress.

The judge looked at

the other dogs.

judge

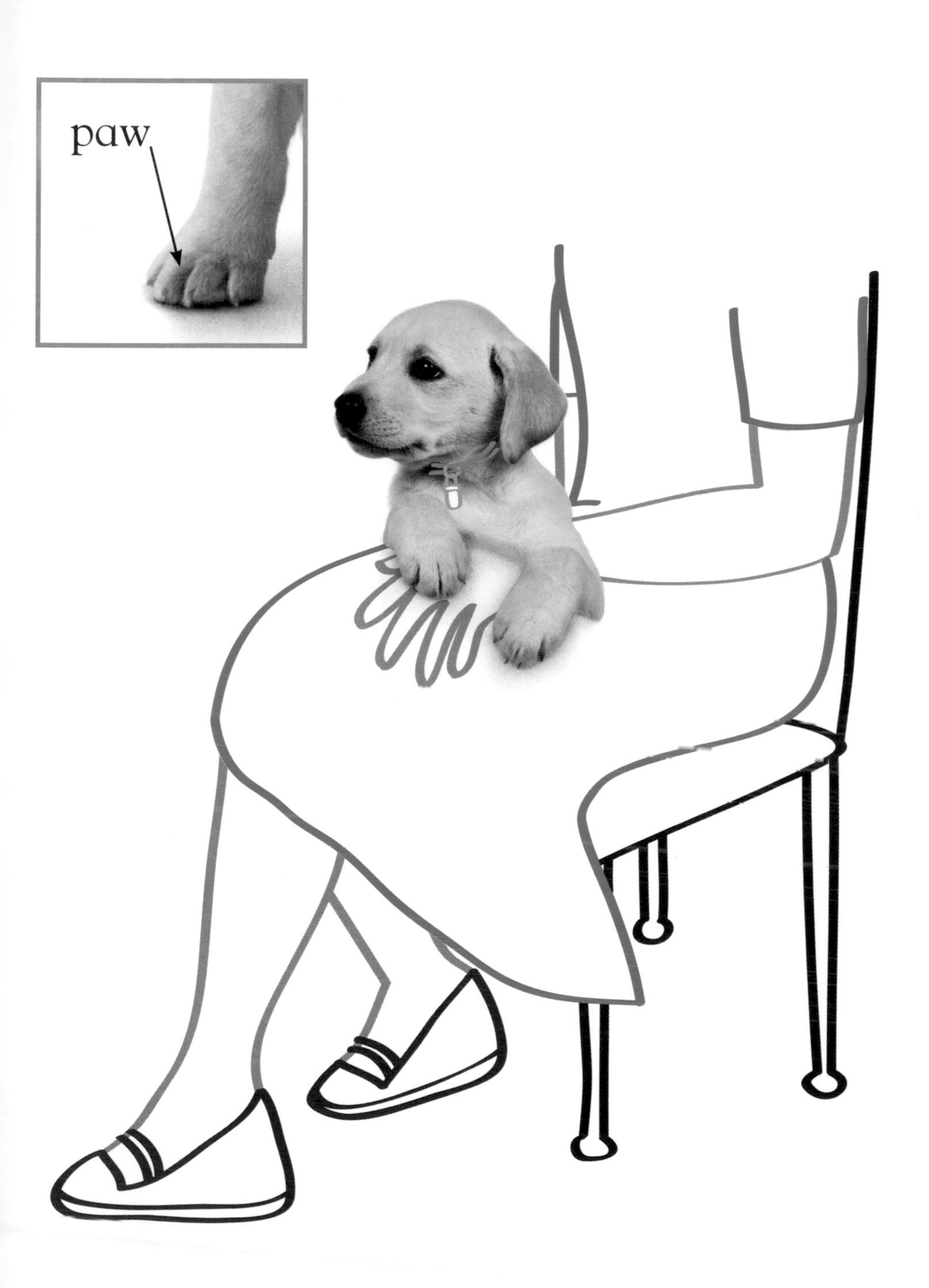
paw

Floppiest ears
Best trick
Longest hair
Fluffiest puppy
Wrinkliest puppy

The prizes were given out

to the winning dogs.

They barked loudly and

wagged their tails.

People clapped and smiled.

Woody looked at Holly

with sad, brown eyes.

Holly stroked his soft,

floppy ears.

"I have one last prize to give out
to a special dog," said the judge.
Who could the winner be?
Everyone stood still.
All was quiet.
The judge said, "The first prize
for the most playful puppy
goes to...

... Woody!"

Holly jumped up and down

in surprise!

Woody's tail began to wag.

He gave Holly a big, wet lick

on her nose.

"Oh, Woody, you really are

the most playful puppy!"

laughed Holly.

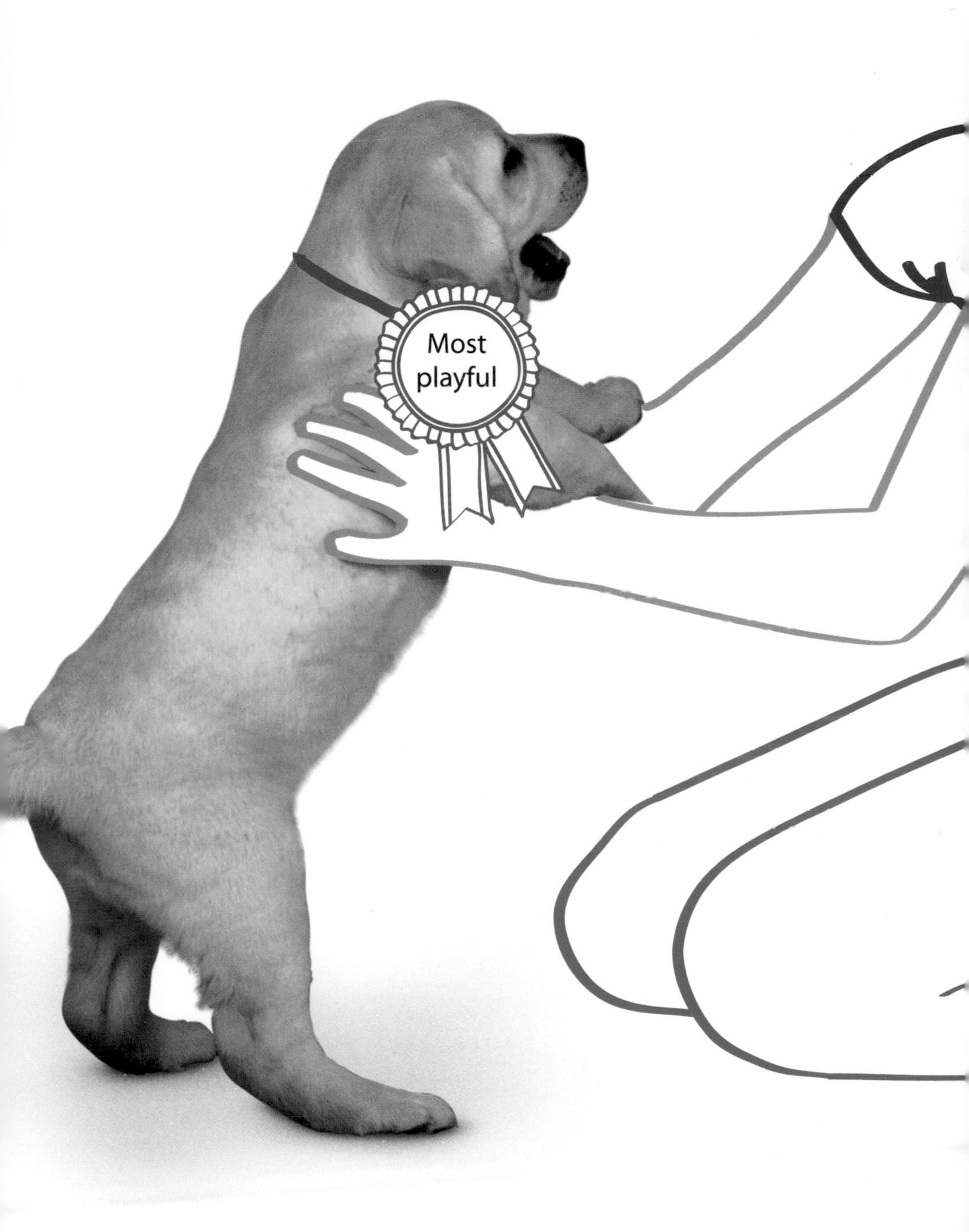
Most
playful

Glossary

Puppy Checklist
This is a checklist of things that are needed for taking care of a puppy.

- [ ] puppy
- [x] puppy food
- [x] bed
- [x] food bowl

Checklist
list of things to be done

Judge
person who chooses the winner

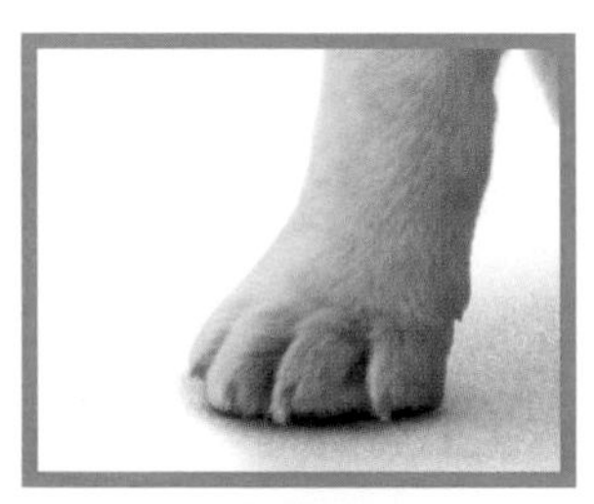

Paw
animal's soft padded foot with claws

Prize
a reward given to a winner of a competition

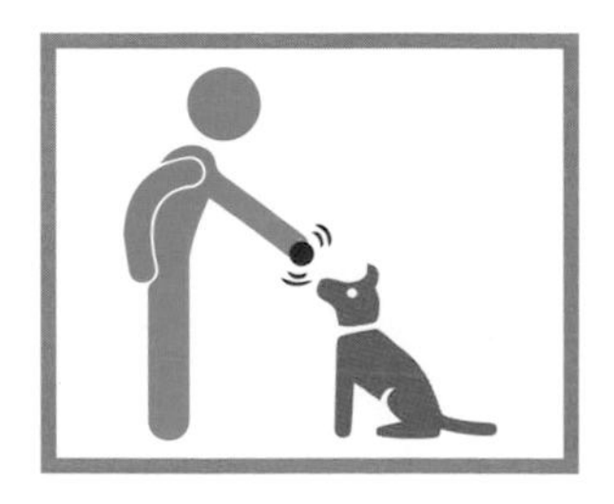

Training
step-by-step teaching to do something new

Index

checklist 5

chew 8

dog show 20

ears 24, 25

fair 19, 20–21

judge 22, 26

jump 6, 16, 22, 28

munch 8

nose 28

paw 23

paw prints 22

pond 16

prizes 21, 25, 26

sit 13

tail 13, 22, 25, 28

town square 19

training 10–11, 13

wagging 13, 22, 25, 28

yard 10, 13, 14

DK READERS help children learn to read, then read to learn. If you enjoyed this DK READER, then look out for these other titles for your child.

Level 1 Deadly Dinosaurs
Roar! Thud! Meet Rexy, Sid, Deano, and Sonia, the dinosaurs that come alive at night in the museum. Who do you think is the deadliest?

Level 1 Little Dolphin
Follow Little Dolphin's adventures when he leaves his mother and joins the older dolphins for the first time. Will he be strong enough to keep up?

Level 1 Bugs Hide and Seek
Surprise! Some bugs have the perfect shape and color to stay hidden. They look like the plants around them. Can you spot them?

Level 1 Mega Machines
Hard hats on! The mega machines are very busy building a new school. Watch them in action!

Level 1 Pirate Attack!
Come and join Captain Blackbeard and his pirate crew for an action-packed adventure on the high seas.